23263

W9-AQQ-522

23263

332.4
Bas

Basel, Roberta.

The history of money

23263

15.95

First Facts™

Learning about Money

The History of Money

by Roberta Basel

Consultant:
Sharon M. Danes, PhD
Professor and Family Economist
University of Minnesota

Capstone press
Mankato, Minnesota

First Facts is published by Capstone Press,
151 Good Counsel Drive, P.O. Box 669, Mankato, Minnesota 56002.
www.capstonepress.com

Library of Congress Cataloging-in-Publication Data
Basel, Roberta.
The history of money / by Roberta Basel.
   p. cm. — (First facts. Learning about money)
   Summary: "Explains how commerce and money have evolved from bartering to currencies
to electronic money"—Provided by publisher.
   Includes bibliographical references and index.
   ISBN-13: 978-0-7368-5396-5 (hardcover)
   ISBN-10: 0-7368-5396-0 (hardcover)
   1. Money—History—Juvenile literature. 2. Commerce—History—Juvenile literature.
I. Title. II. Series.
HG221.5.B295 2006
332.4'9—dc22   2005020622

Editorial Credits
Wendy Dieker, editor; Jennifer Bergstrom, set designer; Bobbi J. Dey, book designer;
   Jo Miller, photo researcher/photo editor

Photo Credits
Brand X Pictures, 5
Capstone Press/Karon Dubke, cover (debit card, US bill, modern coins, shells), 16, 21
Corbis/Bettmann, 6; Charles O'Rear, 11, 20; Owaki-Kulla, 19; Owen Franken, 14
Corel, 8 (bottom left)
Courtesy of MoneyMuseum, cover (Chinese bill, ancient coin), 12–13
The Granger Collection, New York, 8–9 (right)
Photodisc, 8 (top left), 15

1 2 3 4 5 6 11 10 09 08 07 06

Table of Contents

Money

Can you imagine buying food using shells? That's what people did about 10,000 years ago. Shells were one of the earliest kinds of money. Later, money became the bills and coins people still use. Today, people also exchange money on computers. Money has a long history, and it continues to change.

Fun Fact!
Animals, such as sheep, camels, and cows, were also some of the first kinds of money.

6

Bartering

Before they had money, people **bartered** to get things. Bartering was like trading. A person could trade a string of beads to get a basket.

Sometimes, traders didn't have what the other person wanted. People needed items that everyone would take as a trade.

Fun Fact!
Have you ever traded baseball cards? You were bartering!

Metal

Shells

8

Beads

The First Money

Over time, people agreed on items to take in trades. These items were money. Shells, beads, or metal were items that stood for a certain amount.

Sometimes, useful items were used as money. People used sugar, salt, and nails as money.

Fun Fact!

In the 1800s, people in Indonesia used human skulls as money.

9

Coins

Pieces of metal became popular as money. They lasted a long time. But each piece was different. Traders had to weigh the money to check its **worth**.

About 2,500 years ago, the people of Lydia shaped metal into **standard** coins. The coins were worth set amounts. They didn't have to be weighed.

Fun Fact!
The first Lydian coins were bean-shaped lumps. They had a lion's head stamped on them.

Paper Money

The Chinese did not have enough metal to make a lot of coins. They invented paper money about 1,200 years ago. They made the paper from tree bark. Besides being easier to make, paper money was also light and easy to carry.

Fun Fact!
Early Chinese paper money was as big as a piece of notebook paper.

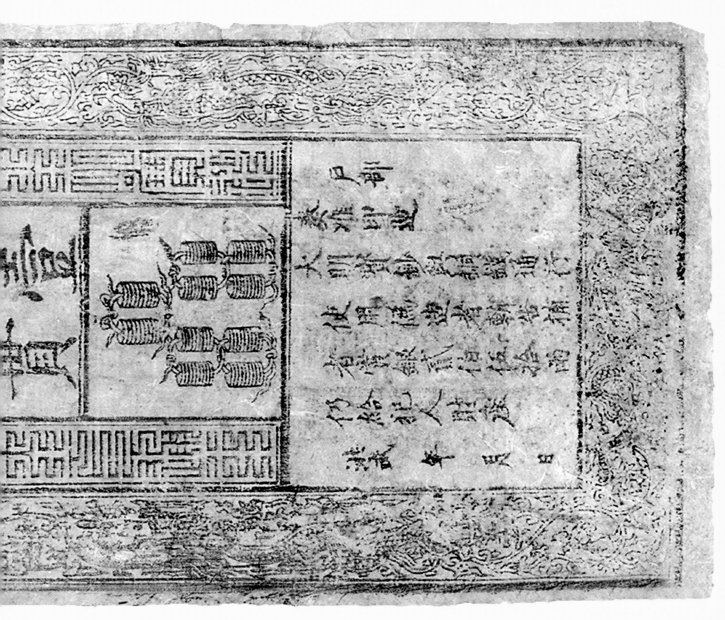

13

Gold Standard

Most countries soon had their own bills and coins. It was hard to spend one country's money in another place. No one knew what it was worth.

Some countries promised their money was worth a certain amount of gold. This promise was the gold standard. It made people trust a country's money.

Banks

Before **banks**, people often hid their money at home. Money wasn't always safe. Banks were built for keeping money safe.

Today, people have bank accounts. Banks keep records of how much money is put in or taken out of **accounts**. These records are kept on computers.

Fun Fact!
The first modern bank in the world opened in Barcelona, Spain, in 1401.

Money Today

Today, using coins and bills isn't the only way to buy things. Checks and **debit cards** let people pay with money in their bank accounts. **Credit cards** let people buy items now and pay for them later. In the future, people might use fingerprints to access their money. What else will the future of money hold?

Fun Fact!

Today, only 8 percent of money is coins and bills. The rest is computer records that stand for money.

Amazing but True!

The heaviest money in the world is on the island of Yap. Huge round stones have holes in the middle so they can be carried on long poles. Some stones stand 12 feet (3.7 meters) tall. They can weigh over 500 pounds (227 kilograms). These stones have been used for hundreds of years.

Hands On: Bartering Game

Before there was money, people bartered to get things.
Play this game with your friends to see how bartering works.

What You Need

2 friends
1 apple
1 banana
1 orange

What You Do

1. Give each person one piece of fruit.
2. Pretend that you each want a different fruit. Trade to get the fruit you each want.
3. Now pretend that one apple is equal to one banana. But one orange is equal to two apples or two bananas. Can everyone trade with the fruit they have?

Who can get the fruit they want? Which of you cannot get the fruit you want? Why doesn't bartering always work?

Glossary

account (uh-KOUNT)—an agreement to keep money in a bank, as in a checking or savings account

bank (BANK)—a business that accepts deposits of money and makes loans

barter (BAR-tur)—to trade for goods and services instead of using money

credit card (KRED-it KARD)—a card used to buy things before paying for them

debit card (DEH-bit KARD)—a card that lets a person use the money from a bank account

standard (STAN-durd)—something that is widely used or accepted as correct

worth (WURTH)—to have a certain value

Read More

Anderson, Jon R. *Money: A Rich History.* Smart about—Money. New York: Grosset & Dunlap, 2003.

Godfrey, Neale S. *Why Money Was Invented.* The One and Only Common Cents Series. Parsippany, N.J.: Silver Press, 1995.

Rosinsky, Natalie M. *All About Money.* Let's See Library. Economics. Minneapolis, Minn.: Compass Point Books, 2004.

Internet Sites

FactHound offers a safe, fun way to find Internet sites related to this book. All of the sites on FactHound have been researched by our staff.

Here's how:
1. Visit *www.facthound.com*
2. Type in this special code **0736853960** for age-appropriate sites. Or enter a search word related to this book for a more general search.
3. Click on the **Fetch It** button.

FactHound will fetch the best sites for you!

Index